Conscious Conversations
Mindful Public Speaking Techniques

Table of Contents

Chapter 1. Introduction

Welcome to a game-changing Special Report on "Conscious Conversations: Mindful Public Speaking Techniques". This is much more than just another guide to effective oratory - it's a refreshing, dynamic blueprint that merges mindfulness techniques with conventional speechcraft. Dive into the exhilaration of public speaking as we shed light on how you can channel self-awareness, intentionality, and presence to enhance your interactions and presentations significantly. Not just for renowned speakers, but virtually anyone striving to improve at interactive communication, our report will revolutionize your speaking journey. Bid adieu to intimidating crowd moments and say hello to masterful, mindful, and engaging public speaking!

Chapter 2. Understanding Conscious Conversations

To unravel the concept of conscious conversations, we need first to dissect it into its two components: consciousness and conversation. Understanding each term individually provides valuable insights into the essence of conscious conversations.

Consciousness, broadly defined, refers to an individual's awareness of their environment, thoughts, and feelings. It entails being present and focused on the present moment rather than being lost in past memories or future predictions. Mindfulness, a closely related concept, involves intentionally directing one's attention to the current experience with an open, curious, and non-judgmental attitude.

Conversations, on the other hand, are interactions through which we exchange ideas, feelings, thoughts, and experiences with others. The goal of a conversation extends beyond conveying information. It also involves understanding the state of mind and emotional context of the other participant(s).

Bringing these components together, a conscious conversation integrates the principles of mindfulness into communication. It entails entering a conversation with conscious intent, remaining present throughout the conversation, and genuinely striving to understand and connect with the other participants on both a cognitive and emotional level.

2.1. The Framework of Conscious Conversations

Conscious conversations are not just about what is being said. They involve much more - understanding the context, regulating emotions, active listening, and responding with empathy. Below, we explore the four foundational pillars of conscious conversations:

1. Mindful Presence: The first step towards conscious conversation is to be thoroughly present. Mindful presence involves focusing your attention on the conversation, actively monitoring your emotions, and ensuring that distractions do not derail you.

2. Active Listening: Listening is as critical in a conversation as speaking. Active listening involves genuinely focusing on the speaker's words, observing non-verbal cues, and refraining from formulating responses while the other party is still speaking.

3. Empathic Understanding: To truly understand another's point of view, you must be able to empathize with their experiences and emotions. Empathic understanding requires suspending your judgments and preconceived notions to appreciate the other's perspective genuinely.

4. Mindful Responding: Mindful responses are intentional, thoughtful, and non-reactive. They involve observing your thoughts and emotions, contemplating your response, and conveying it in a respectful and authentic manner.

2.2. From Mindless to Mindful Conversations

Mindless conversations often follow pre-established scripts or patterns and rarely involve novel, creative, or challenging ideas. They tend to be reactive rather than thoughtful, dominated by automated responses and assumptions. On the other hand, mindful conversations are characterized by originality, depth, and a spirit of discovery and mutual enlightenment.

Moving from mindless to mindful conversations requires practice and patience. Start by observing your conversations and attitudes towards them. Do you find yourself frequently interrupted or distracted during conversations? Are you stuck in automated responses or defensive communication patterns? Do these patterns sidetrack you from the conversation's main topic or prevent you from genuinely understanding the other person's viewpoint?

Once you start becoming aware of these behaviors, you can intentionally work on shifting them to foster more mindful and meaningful conversations. This shift is not a one-time event but an ongoing process that requires continuous self-awareness and self-regulation.

2.3. The Role of Emotional Regulation in Conscious Conversations

Emotions play a crucial role in our conversations. They influence our perspective, shape our responses, and affect the overall communication dynamic. Emotional dysregulation, or the inability to manage one's emotional responses, can lead to reactive conversations characterized by defensiveness, anger, and blame.

Emotional regulation in conscious conversation involves recognizing and accepting your emotions without letting them dominate the conversation. It's not about suppressing or denying your feelings, but understanding them, giving them appropriate attention, and deciding how best to express them in the context of the conversation. This emotional sophistication allows for healthier conversations characterized by empathy, respect, and balanced responses.

2.4. The Impact of Conscious Conversations on Public Speaking

Conscious conversations aren't only applicable to two-way dialogues or small group discussions. They also significantly impact the realm of public speaking, helping you form more meaningful connections with your audience, handle question-and-answer (Q&A) sessions more adeptly, and respond to unexpected occurrences more smoothly.

By embracing the principles of conscious conversations in your public speaking endeavors, you invite your audience into a dialogical space where their insights, experiences, and responses are valued. This dynamic dialogue imbued with mindfulness echoes far beyond the limitations of detached monologues and offers a richer, more fulfilling experience for both you and your audience.

In the midst of the cacophony of countless words spoken daily, conscious conversations stand out. They change the quality of our interactions, deepen our connections with others, and enrich our experiences in personal relationships and public speaking alike. In the next chapters, we'll delve deeper into how you can weave the principles of conscious conversations into your public speaking practice, transforming every stage into a platform for meaningful connection and mutual growth.

Now that you've grasped the concept of conscious conversations, it's time to make the shift. Remember, it's not just about becoming a better speaker but also about engaging more deeply with your audience, understanding their perspectives, and creating meaningful dialogue. So take a deep breath, stay present, and let your journey towards mindful public speaking begin!

Chapter 3. Traverse through the Landscape of Mindfulness

Before embarking on the journey to mastering mindful public speaking, we must first understand mindfulness's vast, enriching landscape. Contrary to popular belief, mindfulness transcends the realm of meditation. It's a profoundly immersive process that enhances every aspect of your life if you practice it diligently.

3.1. The Cornerstones of Mindfulness

Mindfulness essentially consists of two fundamental elements: Awareness and acceptance.

1. **Awareness:** From your thoughts, feelings, bodily sensations, to the environment around you, being aware implies being consciously present to it all. When public speaking, this means being acutely aware of your message, your audience's responses, the tone of your voice, your body language, and more. By strengthening your awareness, you develop an almost palpable rapport with the audience, making your presentation more engaging and authentic.

2. **Acceptance:** This involves a non-judgmental standpoint towards life experiences. It's about finding tranquility amid chaos and handling experiences as they unfold. In public speaking, acceptance would mean not resisting or being anxious about an unforeseen glitch in your presentation, a disengaged audience, or a sudden bout of nervousness. It's about embracing such circumstances and artfully leveraging them to enhance your

speech.

The journey into mindfulness is a deeply personal and transformative one. It's about creating a bond with your inner self and the environment around you.

3.2. The Nature of Mindfulness

Contrary to certain misconceptions, mindfulness isn't a state but a process. It is not reserved for the quiet and tranquil moments of meditation. Mindfulness could be part of every mundane daily activity, from washing dishes, taking a walk, to delivering a captivating speech in front of a packed auditorium.

There are countless paths leading to the oasis of mindfulness, based on one's predispositions and personal preferences. Be it mindfulness meditation, yoga, mindful eating, or Tai Chi; each path holds the potential to guide you towards increased self-awareness and acceptance.

3.3. Mindful Meditations

Mindful meditations are the cornerstone of many individuals' mindfulness journey. They provide a structured approach to develop a heightened sense of self-awareness and acceptance over time. These meditations mainly include:

1. **Mindfulness-Based Stress Reduction (MBSR):** Developed by Dr. Jon Kabat-Zinn at the University of Massachusetts Medical School, MBSR involves a structured eight-week program that incorporates mindfulness meditation, body awareness, yoga, and exploration of patterns of behavior, thinking, feeling and action.

2. **Vipassana:** This form of meditation encourages self-transformation and personal enlightenment through self-observation. Disciples learn to observe the intricate interplay of

their own physical and mental experiences to gain insight into their inner selves.

3. **Loving Kindness Meditation:** By focusing on developing feelings of goodwill, kindness, and warmth towards others, this meditation cultivates a strong bond with other human beings and promotes empathetic communication.

3.4. Physical Manifestations: Yoga and Tai Chi

Yoga and Tai Chi divert from traditional seated meditation, focusing more on coordinating your breathing rhythms with body movements. These practices not only cultivate mindfulness but also improve breathing, flexibility, and physical strength – all beneficial for a robust public-speaking performance.

Yoga encourages mindful movement and deep, controlled breathing – a perfect antidote to panic-induced shallow breathing, commonly experienced by public speakers. Meanwhile, Tai Chi, known as 'meditation in motion,' helps you become more aware of your bodily sensations, promoting a calm demeanor and enhancing overall stage presence.

3.5. Mindful Eating: A Path Less Traveled

Eating is a daily necessity, often performed mechanically. However, turning it into a mindful act can foster an enriched appreciation and understanding of the present moment. Mindful eating involves savoring every bite, slowly and conscientiously, directing your entire focus on the food—the flavors, the textures, the smells, and the act of chewing itself. This practice serves as a perfect grounding exercise strengthening your capacity for mindfulness during public speaking.

As we weave through the diverse landscapes of mindfulness, you'll note that every path eventually leads to the same destination: increased self-awareness and acceptance. The techniques we've explored can contribute significantly to your public speaking journey, allowing you to engage more authentically and effectively with your audience.

The armory of mindfulness doesn't merely dispel the fear of public speaking—it evolves the process into a thrilling, enjoyable act, taking you from being a competent speaker to becoming a mindful orator. Harness the power of mindfulness, and realize the immense potential it holds in transforming your public speaking journey.

Chapter 4. Dynamic Listening: An essential skill

Conversational intelligence doesn't merely rely on the effectiveness of your verbal responses but also on the depth of your dynamic listening. Let's delve into this skill which forms the backbone of effective, mindful public speaking.

4.1. Understanding Dynamic Listening

Dynamic listening, or active listening, is much more than simply hearing the words uttered by someone else. It's a multifaceted skill involving understanding, interpreting, and responding to nuances beyond basic language structures. Dynamic listening not only requires considerable cognitive involvement but also high emotional intelligence. In this section, we will explore what dynamic listening entails and how it impacts public speaking.

Active listening means fully focusing on, understanding, and responding to a speaker in a way that enhances mutual understanding. It's pivotal to developing empathetic connections, which play a key role in effective public speaking. By actively listening to your audience, you can assess their reactions—be it excitement, confusion, or disagreement—and modify your speech accordingly.

4.2. The Components of Dynamic Listening

The practice of dynamic listening brings together several facets, lending it its dynamism. These include non-verbal cues, effective feedback, and avoiding premature judgment.

1. Non-verbal cues: A crucial part of dynamic listening is recognizing and understanding non-verbal cues like body language, eye contact, and others. Non-verbal cues often say much more about a person's thoughts and emotions than their words, so one must be keenly observant to pick up on these signals.

2. Effective feedback: Dynamic listeners not only pay attention to what is being said, but also how they can provide invaluable feedback. They react appropriately to the speaker, often forming a synchronous connection, in turn, facilitating the speaker's performance.

3. Avoiding premature judgment: The listener should be open-minded and refrain from forming premature judgments or interpretations. It's integral to be patient and considerate of the speaker's views, even when they differ from your own.

4.3. The Role of Dynamic Listening in Public Speaking

An effective speaker is always a good listener. As a public speaker, dynamic listening helps you comprehend your audience better and in turn, become an adaptable, engaging orator.

By practicing dynamic listening, you gain insight into the audience's frame of mind, their expectations, reactions, emotions, and more. This helps you tailor your speech to resonate with them, making it more impactful. When your audience sees that you're in tune with their responses, they are more likely to engage and keep the communication channel open.

It is also essential for handling queries and Q&A sessions after your speech. A dynamic listener is able to grasp the crux of the questions properly, give thoughtful answers, and even understand the sentiment behind criticisms, if any, and address them constructively.

4.4. How to Cultivate Dynamic Listening

Cultivating the skill of dynamic listening requires intentional effort and practice. Here are a few actionable steps:

1. Be fully present: Devote your undivided attention to the speaker, filtering out distractions and preoccupations. Remember, being physically present is not enough; mental presence is the true requirement.

2. Acknowledge non-verbal cues: Pay attention to the speaker's body language, facial expressions, gestures, and pause. These cues provide significant insights.

3. Provide visual feedback: Use your own body language to show your engagement. Nod when you understand, or furrow your eyebrows when you're confused. This visual feedback will also help the speaker.

4. Clarify before you respond: If certain points are unclear, don't hesitate to ask for clarification before you respond. This will prevent miscommunication or oversights.

5. Empathy is key: Empathize with your speaker; put yourself in their shoes before responding.

4.5. A Dynamic Listener's Influence on Conversations

Being a dynamic listener can positively influence any conversation, whether you're in a one-on-one chat or addressing thousands of people. Here's how:

1. Builds stronger connections: A good listener demonstrates respect towards the speaker, promoting a better understanding and fostering a more profound connection.

2. Enhances conversation quality: Dynamic listening can help rectify misunderstandings, improve clarity, and deepen the overall essence of a conversation.

3. Cultivates mutual respect: When you actively listen to someone, they feel valued, promoting a sense of mutual respect. This often, in turn, encourages them to become more attentive to your words.

4. Facilitates effective teamwork: In a group or team scenario, dynamic listening fosters effective collaboration, allowing all members' ideas to be heard and respected.

Dynamic listening is more than a public speaking tool. It's a life skill that can drastically transform how you communicate and connect with people. As it roots itself in empathy and understanding, it fosters deeper, more meaningful relationships, not only enhancing public speaking capabilities but also revolutionizing personal conversations.

Chapter 5. Preparation: A Mindful Approach

Understanding the importance of preparation in public speaking cannot be overstated. Most acclaimed orators spend hours, days, even weeks planning prior to stepping onto the dais. However, this preparation surpasses the typical realms of crafting an enticing speech and rehearsals. So, where does the magic of mindfulness come into play in your preparation process? Let's discover!

5.1. Mindful Intent: Crafting Your Speech

Start your journey to mindful public speaking by setting a well-defined intention for your speech. Your intent acts as the cornerstone of your speech, guiding your thoughts and actions throughout your oration. However, setting an intention goes beyond choosing a topic. Mindfulness urges you to ask, "What kind of emotion, thought, or impact do I aim to evoke?"

To sculpt your intention:

1. Select a clear, concise, and actionable objective for your speech.
2. Envision the emotional and psychological landscape you want your audience to traverse.
3. Be authentic in your approach. Let your passion shine through!

This focused intent will assist you in delivering a speech that's coherent and, more importantly, meaningful.

5.2. Research and Relate: Mindful Gathering of Information

Research lies at the heart of any impactful and stimulating speech. But, how can you indulge in mindful research?

1. Immerse yourself entirely in your topic, acknowledging the energy and efforts involved.

2. Understand that every article, book, or documentary you engage with is an exchange of thoughts, ideas, and intelligence.

3. Look for information that resonates with your intention and ethos, not just facts that can wow your audience.

4. Step into the shoes of your audience, recognising the value this information may carry for them.

Mindful research helps in creating a tapestry of knowledge that's comprehensive yet relatable, and academic yet accessible.

5.3. Embrace Vulnerability: Mindful Acceptance of Flaws

One of the vital aspects of mindful communication publicly requires you to acknowledge your fears and flaws instead of fighting them. Accept that it's human nature to experience nervousness or fear of judgement. Analyze these feelings and identify their sources.

Though it may seem counterintuitive, expressing your apprehensions and vulnerabilities can make you more relatable and authentic. However, remember to avoid oversharing unnecessarily, as it can distract the audience.

5.4. Striking a Balance: Mindful Rehearsals

Rehearsing your speech adheres to Parkinson's law - work expands to fill the time available for its completion. Therefore, avoid unlimited rehearsals. Implement mindfulness:

1. Practice in a calm state, focusing on your speech rather than external variables like crowd response or time constraints.

2. Treat each rehearsal like the final delivery, emphasizing each word and expression.

3. Record your sessions to watch your body language, voice modulation, pauses, and other nuances.

Your preparations are incomplete without taking care of your physical well-being, which directly influences your mental state.

5.5. Nourishing Your Body: The Physical Aspects of Preparation

Maintain optimal health to not let your physical state affect performance:

1. Sleep and Rest: Ensure adequate sleep; rest your voice prior to the event.

2. Nutrition: Consume a balanced diet. Avoid heavy meals before your speech; opt for a light snack instead.

3. Exercise: Regular physical activity can help reduce stress and boost confidence.

Through these techniques, preparation for public speaking becomes much more than just poring endlessly over your speech. It transforms into a journey of self-discovery and connection. The magic of mindful preparation prepares you to face not just your audience, but any interaction or situation with a grounded sense of self-assuredness and presence. Embrace this holistic approach to turn public speaking from a source of dread to a source of exhilaration!

Chapter 6. The Art of Articulation: Speaking with Intention

In the realm of public speaking, articulation goes beyond merely stating words clearly and distinctly. It represents a higher level of communication, where your every word carries intention and weight, designed to connect with your audience at a profound level. By integrating mindfulness into articulation, you can achieve more compelling and effective public speaking. This chapter delves into the refined stages of articulation from a mindful perspective. It is a deep exploration into how breathwork, language precision, tonality, and audience connection work hand in hand to create a mindful, personal, and powerful public speaking environment.

6.1. Understanding Articulation: The Cornerstone of Effective Communication

Articulation is the ability to express oneself clearly in both thought and emotion and to have that expression well-received and understood by others. It permeates every field and profession, facilitating positive social interaction, and influencing our capacity to get our message across effectively. In the world of public speaking, articulating with intention becomes much more critical. As a speaker, your word choices and body language must fundamentally resonate with your audience, captivating their attention and igniting their imagination.

6.2. The Power of Mindful Breathing

When applying mindfulness techniques, it is essential to begin by focusing on breathwork. Mindful breathing enables you to retain control over your speech pace and tone, enhancing your articulation capabilities.

Long, deep breaths ahead of delivering your speech can facilitate mental tranquility, improving your ability to concentrate on your message and its delivery. At the same time, this breathing cadence helps in regulating your heart rate, representing a physical manifestation of calmness necessary to ward off any public-speaking nervousness.

6.3. Practicing Precision: Word Choices and Language Use

Being articulate also involves making meticulous word choices and being deliberate with language use. The language you use should align seamlessly with your message, enabling your audience to understand what you're trying to communicate without getting lost in unnecessary or complex jargon.

Precision in language is crucial. Every word you utter should serve a specific purpose. Mindful selection of words demands that a speaker remains in the present moment, basing their choice on the current audience's reactions and the message that needs to be communicated.

6.4. Voice Modulation and Pauses

An intriguing aspect of articulation is tonality. Your voice's tone, speed, and volume significantly influence how your message is perceived, and proper modulation can underscore your words and phrases' relevance.

Mindful public speaking involves consciously using your voice to express emotions tied to your message. A higher pitch might demonstrate excitement, while a slower pace can give the audience time to take in deeper, more profound statements.

Incorporate pauses into your speech to let critical points resonate with your listeners. Used effectively, silence is a potent tool that can make your message more memorable.

6.5. Audience Connection: Articulating with Empathy

An essential part of articulating with intention is forging a strong connection to your audience. This relationship forms by showing empathy, making your speech more than a mere presentation but a conversation with your audience. Understanding your audience's perspectives, their aspirations, and fears will help you tailor your message to resonate better with them.

6.6. Mindfulness Techniques for Improved Articulation

A speaker can enhance their articulation using mindfulness techniques to attune themselves with the present moment completely. Techniques can include focused breathing exercises prior to your speech, grounding exercises to ward off external distractions, or visualization exercises to create mental maps of your speech's flow and audience reactions.

6.7. Embracing Imperfections: Authenticity in Articulation

Embracing the human nature of public speaking contributes significantly to mindful articulation. Rather than aiming for perfection, strive for authenticity. This authenticity induces an approachable atmosphere and fosters a deeper audience connection. Mistakes become learning points that bring you closer to your audience rather than factors that alienate them.

6.8. Conclusion

Mastering the art of articulation is a dynamic process, and when you pair it with mindfulness techniques, it can revolutionize your public speaking abilities. The journey is marked by a series of conscientious decisions, from how you breathe to how you choose to express your thoughts. Remember to stay genuine, connect with your audience, and most importantly, stay in the present moment. In doing so, you'll command attention, respect, and appreciation of any audiences that come your way.

Chapter 7. Stage Presence: Harnessing the Power of Now

The primal understanding about presence, particularly on stage, is accepting that it's less about putting on a persona and more about being your genuine, authentic self. A thoroughly outlined roadmap, punctuated by mindfulness techniques and thought exercises for each avenue of your speaking journey, will help harness the Power of Now.

7.1. Embrace Authenticity

Unmasking your true self begins with embracing authenticity. This revelation is often arrived at after meticulous introspection. Acknowledge your strengths, weaknesses, fears - everything that make you, You.

Start by making a list of all the unique qualities you possess. It doesn't have to be directly related to public speaking. Any characteristic that defines who you are can make it to that list. Reflect on each and think about how it can influence your speaking style. By doing this, you inch closer to becoming a speaker who is unafraid to showcase their personality, ultimately enhancing your captivating stage presence.

7.2. Self-Awareness: Your Inner Compass

Next, we navigate the depths of self-awareness, an integral aspect of mindful public speaking. It's like an inner compass that cues you when you are veering off your authentic path. Mindfulness exercises such as meditation and guided imagery can be potent mechanisms for enhancing self-awareness.

A simple mindfulness exercise to begin the day is: Sit comfortably and close your eyes. Focus on your breath, following its rhythm as it ebbs and flows. If your thoughts wander, gently bring them back to your breath. This little routine enhances the connection with your inner self, elucidating your speaking style and communication mannerisms over time.

7.3. Power of Intentionality

Taking center stage envelops more than just delivering your side of the story. It includes making the audience a part of it as well. Cultivating the power of intentionality allows you to project your purpose, your passion to the audience such that they not just hear your words, but feel them too.

Begin your preparation with a clear vision of what you wish to impart — consider this your speech's 'soul'. Every word, every phrase should align to this intention.

7.4. Own the Stage

Now, emboldened by authenticity, led by your inner compass, and driven by your intentionality, it's time to own the stage. Stage presence isn't about dominating the platform but about exuding confidence, eloquence, and empathy, making the audience feel welcome, keeping them riveted to your words.

Fear and apprehension tend to make speakers stick to the podium. Break free! Use the stage, move around; this creates a dynamic, engaging atmosphere. Connect with your audience via storytelling, anecdotes, or personal experiences. Make your speech an immersive experience rather than a monologue.

Remember, the spotlight is not a monster. It's a beacon guiding you and the audience through the enriching journey of your speech.

7.5. Channeling the "Now"

Stage presence is intrinsically tied to existing in the "now", staying alert, and responsive to the present moment. Avoid thinking about impending slides or topics. Let the mindfulness techniques, honed over time, come to your rescue.

Perhaps nothing is as illuminating as watching a droplet of water falling into a pond in your mind's eye, creating ripples that spread across, only to give way to the calm again – pivotal wisdom about cause, effect, and peace. Such thought exercises help you stay tuned to the present moment, allowing you to dynamically respond to the room's mood, making you a more engaging speaker.

7.6. Feedback Loop

Lastly, never underestimate the power of reflection and feedback. Constructive feedback can be a powerful tool for personal growth and should be actively sought after each presentation. Self-reflection is equally important to identify areas of improvement.

And remember, while feedback is key, do not lose yourself in the process. Reiterate your positivities, work on your negatives, but stay well grounded in the authentic self, the present experience - this is the essence of commanding stage presence.

In conclusion, stage presence is less about theatrics and more about the genuine connection it fosters between you and the audience. A perfect blend of authenticity, self-awareness, intentionality, owned energy, existence in the "Now", and reflection; it's assured to endow upon you a palpable and transformative command over mindful public speaking. So, immerse yourself in this insightful journey of self-discovery and master the art of stage presence, harnessing the power of Now!

Chapter 8. Storytelling: A Mindful Path to Connection

"Once upon a time..." - three simple words that have been used to deliver stories that have lived through generations. Timeless stories have the power to paint pictures in our minds, connect us emotionally and create a bond of understanding that transcends language and culture.

But storytelling is not limited to tales told around a campfire or bedtime stories in the stillness of the night. In the realm of public speaking, storytelling plays a crucial role, as it offers a vehicle to connect speaker to the audience at a deep, empathetic level.

8.1. Merging Mindfulness With Storytelling

Mindfulness and storytelling share a common thread – they both invite us into the present moment. Where storytelling draws listeners into the immersive world of the narrative, mindfulness brings the speaker into the immediate here and now, creating a solid platform from which the story can arise and be delivered.

The true marriage of mindfulness and storytelling lies in the power of focused attention. As the speaker, you are first and foremost a storyteller. When you merge that role with the practice of mindfulness, focus is heightened, clarity is magnified, and the ability to evoke emotions is sharpened. This potent combination allows you to deliver your tale in a way that not only captures but also mesmerizes your audience.

8.2. Building Blocks of Mindful Storytelling

The art of mindful storytelling entails many elements. Consider them not just building blocks, but contributors to the overall harmony: structuring your story, setting the scene, creating characters, and building narrative tension. Let's delve deeper:

1. **Structure:** A clear and solid structure is a necessary foundation. Every story consists of three basic parts: the beginning, middle, and end. Your tale should also have a clear conflict that the narrative ultimately resolves.

2. **Setting:** Use the five senses to create vivid and relatable settings in the minds of your listeners. Be mindful of the details you include to construct a rich tapestry.

3. **Characters:** The people (or organisms or objects) in your story must be well-rounded, possess depth, and be relatable to your audience. By exploring their thoughts, feelings, and reactions, you allow your listeners to connect emotionally.

4. **Conflict:** A great story requires a compelling conflict. By generating tension, you capture the audience's attention, marooning them on the edge of their seats as they eagerly anticipate the resolution.

8.3. The Power of Three

An essential aspect of storytelling is the rule of three. This simple but effective method makes your story easier to remember and adds an engaging rhythm to your tale. Drilling down deeper, the pattern of setup (1), confrontation (2), and resolution (3) is a formula that has stood the test of time. Entertainment, education, and engagement all rolled into one simple rule.

8.4. Perfecting the Art of Pausing

One of the most underused yet vital storytelling tools is the pause. A moment of silence can achieve dramatic effect, allow the audience to reflect, and give you time to gather your thoughts. Moreover, a well-placed pause can steer and alter the emotional tone of your storytelling. Practice mindful silences, experiment with their duration, and watch as your story ebb and flow with enhanced dynamism.

8.5. Practicing Mindful Storytelling

Just as mindfulness must be cultivated, so must mindful storytelling. Take the time to practice your narrative skills with mindfulness at the forefront. Incorporate mindfulness meditation into your preparation. Just fifteen minutes a day can increase your focus, decrease anxiety, and improve your ability to deliver your tale with authenticity and connection. Practice storytelling, too; share anecdotes with friends and family and take note of what captures their attention.

8.6. The Lasting Impact of Mindful Storytelling

Stories have the power to shift perspectives, shape values, and mobilize action. By combining storytelling with mindfulness, you will discover a transformative path— transforming not only your own public speaking capabilities but also profoundly impacting your listeners.

To the audience, a story delivered mindfully is a delightful experience, like a delicately crafted feast that nourishes their desire for engagement, connection, and shared experience. Slowly but surely, you become more than just a speaker standing on a stage -

you become a person sharing a transformative moment with every individual.

Mindful storytelling offers a simple yet profound shift in the way we give speeches and presentations. It transcends stuffy boardrooms and sterile podiums, inviting instead a shared journey of reflection, insight, and deep connection. By putting this powerful technique into practice, you allow your words to truly touch hearts, stimulate minds, and inspire change.

Chapter 9. Overcoming Public Speaking Anxiety

Studio lights, a sea of expectant faces, deafening silence—public speaking anxiety frequently stems from such intense and challenging situations that might daunt even the most seasoned speakers. However, mindfulness techniques present an avenue towards more confident, successful public communication.

9.1. Understanding Public Speaking Anxiety

Public speaking anxiety, or glossophobia, as it is scientifically termed, is a specific type of social phobia characterized by an intense fear of speaking in public. It's completely normal to feel jittery before a big performance or presentation. However, when fear begins to impact your performance significantly or even prevents you from speaking publicly, it becomes an issue that requires addressing.

This fear usually manifests itself through a series of physical symptoms such as palpitations, sweating, tremors, a dry mouth, or even gastrointestinal discomfort. It may also feature psychological symptoms like excessive worry, negative thoughts, or feelings of panic.

9.2. The Role of Mindfulness in Alleviating Anxiety

Mindfulness can be defined as a sort of meditative state where one focuses entirely on the present moment, acknowledging and accepting one's emotions and thoughts without any judgment. By incorporating mindfulness, it becomes easier to understand your anxious feelings and eventually gain control over them.

9.3. Mindfulness Techniques for Anxiety Management

There are several mindfulness techniques that can be inserted into your public speaking routine to manage anxiety.

1. **Mindful Breathing**: This involves paying close attention to your breath, breathing slowly, and deeply, keeping your mind focused on each inhale and exhale. This practice helps to lower the heart rate and promote relaxation.

2. **Progressive Muscle Relaxation (PMR)**: This involves tensing and then releasing each muscle group in your body, starting from your toes and working up to your forehead. As you tense and relax each muscle group, you bring awareness to your physical sensations and promote overall relaxation.

3. **Mindfulness Meditation**: This involves sitting quietly and focusing on your natural breathing or on a word or mantra that you repeat silently. Allow thoughts to come and go without judgment and return to your focus on breath or mantra.

4. **Visualization**: Visualization, or guided imagery, involves creating peaceful and positive images in your mind to replace negative or anxious thoughts.

9.4. Putting Mindfulness Techniques into Practice

To harness these mindfulness techniques, a regular practice routine is essential. Just as you would rehearse your speech, rehearse mindfulness.

Step 1 - Starting with your natural, quiet breathing, progressively deepen your breaths, focusing your entire attention on this.

Step 2 - After calming your breath, bring your focus to your body sensations. Notice the feeling of your attire against your skin, the ground beneath your feet or the chair supporting your weight.

Step 3 - Apply progressive muscle relaxation to each of your muscle groups, starting at your feet and working your way up to your head.

Step 4 - Use visualization to picture yourself delivering your speech with success.

Step 5 - Finally, practice speaking your speech. Start from conversational to a formal mode of delivery, while maintaining mindfulness throughout.

9.5. Modifying Mindset and Expectations

Reframe your perception of public speaking from a high-stakes pressure situation to an opportunity for sharing information and connecting with others. By adjusting your perspective and expectations from a performance-based endeavor to an interaction-based practice, you can significantly decrease your anxiety levels.

9.6. Handling Anxiety in the Moment

If the stage fright hits just as you're about to speak, take a moment to ground yourself in your environment. Try the 5-4-3-2-1 grounding technique where you identify five things you can see, four things you can touch, three things you can hear, two things you can smell, and one thing you can taste.

9.7. Incorporating Mindful Speaking Techniques

Mindful speaking involves focusing on the message you want to convey and the process of delivering it, rather than on self-conscious thoughts. Remember that your audience is there to listen to what you have to say, not to find faults in your presentation.

9.8. Mindful Listening

Mindful listening is the process of fully receiving what the other person is saying, free from judgment or distraction. Listening mindfully during question and answer sessions allows you to provide thoughtful responses and maintain a connection with your audience.

Incorporating mindfulness into your public speaking routine not only helps you manage anxiety, but also improve your overall speaking skills. With time and consistent practice, you can transform your public speaking journey, embracing the exhilarating thrill it offers rather than shying away from fear. Wake up to the power of mindful public speaking and wave goodbye to glossophobia - your audience awaits!

Chapter 10. Nurturing Authenticity in your Speech

The ebbing curiosity tide of human communication has continually underscored one essential element: the compelling value of authenticity. Authenticity in speech elicits respect, fosters credibility, and forges meaningful connections with listeners.

To peek behind the veil of authenticity, understand its framework, and glean actionable insights, we explore its multiple facets in this transformative journey towards conscious conversations.

10.1. Understanding Authenticity

In its essence, authenticity connotes embracing and projecting your most genuine self, unclouded by pretense or artifice. It is the courage to be vulnerable, to be you, unwavering as the tides of public opinion ebb and flow. Authenticity in speech, then, isn't about posturing or performing; instead, it is about expressing your honest thoughts, emotions, and experiences.

10.2. The Fundamental Pillars of Authentic Speech

To craft an authentic speech effectively, it's crucial to reiterate its three fundamental pillars - truthfulness, vulnerability, and empathy.

1. **Truthfulness:** Truthfulness sets the foundation for authenticity, embedded in factual accuracy and genuine beliefs, perspectives, or emotions. Authentic speech entails speaking the truth, both literally and metaphorically. It calls for an accurate reflection of facts, but also for candidly projecting your comprehension and emotions related to the subject matter.

2. **Vulnerability:** If truthfulness is the foundation of authenticity, vulnerability is its underpinning essence. Vulnerability isn't about exposing weaknesses; rather, it epitomizes the courage to acknowledge that you may not have all the answers, the boldness to make mistakes, and the willingness to share personal anecdotes or emotions that resonate with the audience.

3. **Empathy:** Empathy binds authenticity with a golden thread, interlinking your self-expression with the emotions, experiences, and perspectives of others. It means sensitively tailoring your communication to resonate with your listeners, weaving a shared tapestry of human experiences and emotions.

10.3. Embodying the Pillars of Authentic Speech

Now that we've understood the basic pillars, let's delve deeper to explore how we can embody these into our speeches.

10.4. Crafting Truthful Narratives

Authenticity in speech begins with drafting truthful narratives. First and foremost, ensure factual integrity. Any misrepresentation or exaggeration can significantly erode your credibility and authenticity.

However, being truthful is not just about factual accuracy, but also about presenting your genuine emotions, perspectives, and experiences with the topic under discussion. It's about not shying away from expressing your opinions, even when they are contrary to the popular narrative.

10.5. Embracing Vulnerability

Vulnerability is a potent tool that can remarkably enhance the authenticity of your interaction. Share personal anecdotes and experiences, express your doubts and uncertainties, and show willingness to learn and unlearn.

Give your audience a glimpse behind the scenes, share the journey leading up to your current understanding, and express your openness to evolving perspectives. This combination of personalization and humility humanizes you, thereby fostering a deep connection with the audience.

10.6. Cultivating Empathy

To cultivate empathy, start with understanding your audience. Research their backgrounds, interests, and perspectives. Deeply acknowledging the audience's sensibilities can help tailor your speech to resonate emotionally with them.

In empathetic communication, the language, examples, and stories should mirror the experiences, emotions, and viewpoints of the audience. This empathetic mirroring can foster deep-rooted connections, enhance understanding, and bolster the impact of your speech.

10.7. Bridging the Gap between Authenticity and Audience reception

While authenticity is inherently personal, ensuring its effective transmission to your audience merits cognizance. Tailoring the dissemination of authentic speech to various audience types and contexts is paramount.

10.8. Engaging Audiences with Authenticity

The manner in which your authenticity is received pivots significantly on effective audience engagement. Employ a variety of narrative tools—such as stories, analogies, humor, and questions—to make your authentic content engaging.

Involve the audience in your narrative journey. This involvement can take the form of asking open-ended questions, inviting audience experiences, or interactive activities that deliver your message in an engaging way.

10.9. Adapting Authenticity to Different Contexts

While authenticity is universal, each context calls for a unique adaptation. For instance, while an inspirational talk may benefit from a deep dive into personal experiences, a technical presentation might demand transparency regarding your expertise level and the source of your information.

Understanding the specific demands of each context and adapting your authenticity accordingly can enhance the significance and effectiveness of your communication.

10.10. Wrapping Up

Nurturing authenticity in your speech is a constant process of exploring the self, accepting vulnerability, empathizing with the audience, and adapting to varying contexts. While this task may seem daunting, the rewards are tremendous. Engaging your listeners with authenticity not only amplifies the impact of your message but also paves the way for profound, transformative interactions. Embrace this journey, continue to grow, and harness the power of being your unique, authentic self. Together, let's revolutionize the landscape of interactive communication, one conscious conversation at a time.

Chapter 11. Final Thoughts: Conscious Speaking as a Way of Life

Surrounding ourselves with an invisible bubble of the tranquillity of mindfulness is a wonderful start, yet conscious speaking carries more transformative potential when imbibed as an everyday practice. It flows beyond the platforms and podiums, manifesting in every sector of life - be it a regular team meeting at work, an animated conversation with acquaintances, or a connective dialogue with a loved one. It is a journey that leads you toward growing self-awareness, an improved ability to 'tune in' to others, and increased command of narrative techniques to bolster your points, narratives or stories.

11.1. Embracing Conscious Speaking: Road to Habit Formation

Imprinting any skill into our neural networks—transforming it into a habit—requires patience and calculated effort. It's almost akin to chipping at an 'unconscious communication' statue to reveal a 'conscious speaker' layer by nuanced layer. And sustaining this practice in your everyday interactions is central to this personal transformation.

Begin by relishing the present moment in all communications. Become conscious of your thoughts, your words, the listener's response, and the environment. Let no stimuli go unnoticed. Exercising mindfulness begets clarity, and clarity, in turn, fosters an effective connection with your audience. Pacing your conversations, perhaps with pauses, can yield wonders as it can help gather thoughts and grant the listener a moment to assimilate them.

Besides, keep mixing and matching your mindfulness techniques and public speaking skills. Remember, this journey emerges from the fusion of two domains, not just one. So keep the duo in sync and grow organically. For instance, practice quick mindfulness exercises even before informal conversations, or manage stage anxiety using guided visualisation of a positive reaction from the crowd.

Despite the challenges, celebrate the little victories. Maybe you felt more composed during a stressful situation or perceived an improvement in commanding the attention of your audience. Every single step forward is a testament to your progress.

11.2. A Lifelong Pursuit: Continuous Learning

Conscious speaking is more of a journey than a destination; it's about embracing the mindset of continuous learning and growth. It's not about becoming 'perfect' - it is about committing to evolve, to be better than you were before.

Keep evolving in this craft by constantly updating yourself with newer insights in mindfulness, communication science and public speaking techniques. Attending workshops, collaborating with like-minded individuals, challenging your comfort zones can create varied avenues of progress.

Moreover, don't hesitate to seek feedback. It can prove invaluable in identifying blind spots or areas of improvement. Be open to accept both praise and criticism. Remember, the objective is evolution, not validation.

11.3. Trickle-Down Impact: Transformative Power of Conscious Speaking

Mastering conscious communication doesn't just improve your speaking skills or your ability to keep a listener engaged. It rewires the brain to be more compassionate, understanding, and respectful. By simply being more present in conversations, you foster meaningful relationships.

Look at larger speeches or more significant events as vessels of energy. The kind of energy you imbibe during preparation and exude during the event establishes the event's 'mood'. When conscious speaking underpins your preparation and delivery, imagine the sheer amount of positivity and focus you transmit. It goes beyond just effective communication, dabbling into creating an impact at a macroscopic level – a ripple effect starting from you and reaching far and wide.

11.4. Consciously Speaking beyond Oratory

While the context so far has been leaning towards public speaking, remember, conscious communication permeates every aspect of human interaction. The same principles apply in a one-on-one conversation with a friend, during a difficult negotiation at work, or a stimulating discussion at a social gathering.

The 'stage' isn't always a platform facing a large crowd. It's essentially the environment where you're conveying your thoughts. And being present and conscious on each of these 'stages' enhances your social encounters, making you more receptive and respected as a communicator.

By adhering to the principles and practices shared throughout the report, and by becoming more mindful about your daily communication, you can transition from a casual speaker to a truly compelling conversationalist who knows the beauty of conscious speaking; weaving mindfulness into everyday conversations.

In conclusion, the pursuit of conscious communication is not about being the most charismatic or eloquent speaker, but about becoming a more self-aware, intentional, empathetic, and effective communicator in all spheres of life.

Embrace this mindfulness-infused way of communicating, transform not just the way you speak, but also the way you connect, listen and relate to the world around you. Rest assured, this journey of conscious speaking as a way of life will fruitfully revolutionize your entire speaking journey and beyond. You'd be surprised to discover the profound changes it can incite, not just in your speaking engagements, but in your overall approach to interactions, relationships, and life itself. So embark, persevere and evolve – it's time to let your voice resound as the voice of a conscious speaker!

www.ingramcontent.com/pod-product-compliance
Lightning Source LLC
Chambersburg PA
CBHW062304290526
45794CB00006B/2686